Exposure Draft

Amendments to IFRS 17

Comments to be received by 25 September 2019

Exposure Draft ED/2019/4 *Amendments to IFRS 17* is published by the IFRS Foundation (Foundation).

ISBN for this part: 978-1-911629-33-7

ISBN for complete publication (two parts): 978-1-911629-32-0

CONTENTS

Introduction

Reasons for this Exposure Draft

This Exposure Draft, published by the International Accounting Standards Board (Board), proposes targeted amendments to IFRS 17 *Insurance Contracts* (issued in May 2017) to respond to concerns and challenges raised by stakeholders as IFRS 17 is being implemented.

IFRS 17 is needed to address many inadequacies in the wide range of insurance accounting practices used applying IFRS 4 *Insurance Contracts* and significant implementation activities are already underway. The Board has considered the concerns and challenges raised by stakeholders and concluded that the potential costs of proposing targeted amendments to IFRS 17 could be justified if those amendments would provide meaningful support to entities implementing the Standard and if those amendments:

(a) would not change the fundamental principles of the Standard because that would result in a significant loss of useful information for users of financial statements relative to that which would otherwise result from applying IFRS 17; and

(b) would avoid unduly disrupting implementation already under way or risking undue delays in the effective date of IFRS 17.

Proposals in this Exposure Draft

This Exposure Draft proposes targeted amendments to IFRS 17 relating to the following topics:

(a) scope exclusions—credit card contracts and loan contracts that meet the definition of an insurance contract (paragraphs 7(h), 8A, Appendix D and BC9–BC30);

(b) expected recovery of insurance acquisition cash flows (paragraphs 28A–28D, 105A –105C, B35A–B35C and BC31–BC49);

(c) contractual service margin attributable to investment-return service and investment-related service (paragraphs 44-45, 109 and 117(c)(v), Appendix A, paragraphs B119–B119B and BC50–BC66);

(d) reinsurance contracts held—recovery of losses on underlying insurance contracts (paragraphs 62, 66A–66B, B119C–B119F and BC67–BC90);

(e) presentation in the statement of financial position (paragraphs 78–79, 99, 132 and BC91–BC100);

(f) applicability of the risk mitigation option (paragraphs B116 and BC101–BC109);

(g) effective date of IFRS 17 and the IFRS 9 *Financial Instruments* temporary exemption in IFRS 4 (paragraph C1, [Draft] Amendments to IFRS 4 and paragraphs BC110–BC118);

(h) transition modifications and reliefs (paragraphs C3(b), C5A, C9A, C22A and BC119–BC146); and

(i) minor amendments (see paragraphs BC147–BC163).

The Basis for Conclusions explains the Board's rationale for the proposed amendments in this Exposure Draft. The Basis for Conclusions also explains the Board's rationale for other amendments the Board considered and decided not to propose (paragraphs BC164–BC220). Paragraph BC221 of the Basis for Conclusions summarises the likely costs and benefits of the proposed amendments.

Who would be affected by the proposals in this Exposure Draft?

The proposed amendments could affect any entity that issues insurance contracts within the scope of IFRS 17.

When would the proposals be effective?

This Exposure Draft proposes that entities would be required to apply the amended Standard for annual reporting periods beginning on or after 1 January 2022.

Next steps

The Board will consider comments it receives on the Exposure Draft before 25 September 2019 and will decide whether to proceed with the proposed amendments to IFRS 17. The Board plans to publish any resulting amendments to IFRS 17 in mid-2020.

Although further implementation issues could arise, the Board expects that any further issues would be unlikely to lead to further standard-setting. Stakeholders have had a significant amount of time since the issuance of IFRS 17 to identify substantive implementation issues and the Board expects any such issues to have already been identified. In addition, recognising that any further changes to IFRS 17 are more likely to disrupt rather than help the implementation process, the Board is reluctant to propose further amendments until after the Post-implementation Review of IFRS 17.

Invitation to comment

The Board invites comments on the Exposure Draft *Amendments to IFRS 17*, particularly on the questions set out below. Comments are most helpful if they:

(a) respond to the questions as stated;

(b) indicate the specific paragraph or paragraphs to which they relate;

(c) contain a clear rationale; and

(d) identify any wording in the proposals that is difficult to translate.

The Board is requesting comments only on matters addressed in this Exposure Draft.

Questions for respondents

Question 1—Scope exclusions—credit card contracts and loan contracts that meet the definition of an insurance contract (paragraphs 7(h), 8A, Appendix D and BC9–BC30)

(a) Paragraph 7(h) proposes that an entity would be required to exclude from the scope of IFRS 17 credit card contracts that meet the definition of an insurance contract if, and only if, the entity does not reflect an assessment of the insurance risk associated with an individual customer in setting the price of the contract with that customer.

Do you agree with the proposed amendment? Why or why not?

(b) If not excluded from the scope of IFRS 17 by paragraphs 7(a)–(h), paragraph 8A proposes that an entity would choose to apply IFRS 17 or IFRS 9 to contracts that meet the definition of an insurance contract but limit the compensation for insured events to the amount required to settle the policyholder's obligation created by the contract (for example, loans with death waivers). The entity would be required to make that choice for each portfolio of insurance contracts, and the choice for each portfolio would be irrevocable.

Do you agree with the proposed amendment? Why or why not?

Question 2—Expected recovery of insurance acquisition cash flows (paragraphs 28A–28D, 105A–105C, B35A–B35C and BC31–BC49)

Paragraphs 28A–28D and B35A–B35C propose that an entity:

(a) allocate, on a systematic and rational basis, insurance acquisition cash flows that are directly attributable to a group of insurance contracts to that group and to any groups that include contracts that are expected to arise from renewals of the contracts in that group;

(b) recognise as an asset insurance acquisition cash flows paid before the group of insurance contracts to which they are allocated is recognised; and

(c) assess the recoverability of an asset for insurance acquisition cash flows if facts and circumstances indicate the asset may be impaired.

Paragraphs 105A–105C propose disclosures about such assets.

Do you agree with the proposed amendments? Why or why not?

Question 3—Contractual service margin attributable to investment-return service and investment-related service (paragraphs 44–45, 109 and 117(c)(v), Appendix A, paragraphs B119–B119B and BC50–BC66)

(a) Paragraphs 44, B119–B119A and the definitions in Appendix A propose that an entity identify coverage units for insurance contracts without direct participation features considering the quantity of benefits and expected period of investment-return service, if any, in addition to insurance coverage. Paragraph B119B specifies criteria for when contracts may provide an investment-return service.

Do you agree with the proposed amendment? Why or why not?

(b) Paragraphs 45, B119–B119A and the definitions in Appendix A clarify that an entity is required to identify coverage units for insurance contracts with direct participation features considering the quantity of benefits and expected period of both insurance coverage and investment-related service.

Do you agree with the proposed amendment? Why or why not?

(c) Paragraph 109 proposes that an entity disclose quantitative information about when the entity expects to recognise in profit or loss the contractual service margin remaining at the end of a reporting period. Paragraph 117(c)(v) proposes an entity disclose the approach used to determine the relative weighting of the benefits provided by insurance coverage and investment-return service or investment-related service.

Do you agree with the proposed disclosure requirements? Why or why not?

Question 4—Reinsurance contracts held—recovery of losses on underlying insurance contracts (paragraphs 62, 66A–66B, B119C–B119F and BC67–BC90)
Paragraph 66A proposes that an entity adjust the contractual service margin of a group of reinsurance contracts held that provides proportionate coverage, and as a result recognise income, when the entity recognises a loss on initial recognition of an onerous group of underlying insurance contracts, or on addition of onerous contracts to that group. The amount of the adjustment and resulting income is determined by multiplying: (a) the loss recognised on the group of underlying insurance contracts; and (b) the fixed percentage of claims on the group of underlying contracts the entity has a right to recover from the group of reinsurance contracts held. Do you agree with the proposed amendment? Why or why not?

Question 5—Presentation in the statement of financial position (paragraphs 78–79, 99, 132 and BC91–BC100)
The proposed amendment to paragraph 78 would require an entity to present separately in the statement of financial position the carrying amount of portfolios of insurance contracts issued that are assets and those that are liabilities. Applying the existing requirements, an entity would present the carrying amount of groups of insurance contracts issued that are assets and those that are liabilities. The amendment would also apply to portfolios of reinsurance contracts held that are assets and those that are liabilities. Do you agree with the proposed amendment? Why or why not?

Question 6—Applicability of the risk mitigation option (paragraphs B116 and BC101–BC109)
The proposed amendment to paragraph B116 would extend the risk mitigation option available when an entity uses derivatives to mitigate financial risk arising from insurance contracts with direct participation features. That option would apply in circumstances when an entity uses reinsurance contracts held to mitigate financial risk arising from insurance contracts with direct participation features. Do you agree with the proposed amendment? Why or why not?

Question 7—Effective date of IFRS 17 and the IFRS 9 temporary exemption in IFRS 4 (paragraphs C1, [Draft] Amendments to IFRS 4 and BC110–BC118)

IFRS 17 is effective for annual reporting periods beginning on or after 1 January 2021. The amendments proposed in this Exposure Draft are such that they should not unduly disrupt implementation already under way or risk undue delays in the effective date.

(a) The proposed amendment to paragraph C1 would defer the effective date of IFRS 17 by one year from annual reporting periods beginning on or after 1 January 2021 to annual reporting periods beginning on or after 1 January 2022.

Do you agree with the proposed amendment? Why or why not?

(b) The proposed amendment to paragraph 20A of IFRS 4 would extend the temporary exemption from IFRS 9 by one year so that an entity applying the exemption would be required to apply IFRS 9 for annual reporting periods beginning on or after 1 January 2022.

Do you agree with the proposed amendment? Why or why not?

Question 8—Transition modifications and reliefs (paragraphs C3(b), C5A, C9A, C22A and BC119–BC146)

(a) Paragraph C9A proposes an additional modification in the modified retrospective approach. The modification would require an entity, to the extent permitted by paragraph C8, to classify as a liability for incurred claims a liability for settlement of claims incurred before an insurance contract was acquired.

Paragraph C22A proposes that an entity applying the fair value approach could choose to classify such a liability as a liability for incurred claims.

Do you agree with the proposed amendments? Why or why not?

(b) The proposed amendment to paragraph C3(b) would permit an entity to apply the option in paragraph B115 prospectively from the transition date, rather than the date of initial application. The amendment proposes that to apply the option in paragraph B115 prospectively on or after the transition date, an entity would be required to designate risk mitigation relationships at or before the date it applies the option.

Do you agree with the proposed amendment? Why or why not?

(c) Paragraph C5A proposes that an entity that can apply IFRS 17 retrospectively to a group of insurance contracts be permitted to instead apply the fair value approach to that group if it meets specified criteria relating to risk mitigation.

Do you agree with the proposed amendment? Why or why not?

Question 9—Minor amendments (BC147–BC163)
This Exposure Draft also proposes minor amendments (see paragraphs BC147–BC163 of the Basis for Conclusions). Do you agree with the Board's proposals for each of the minor amendments described in this Exposure Draft? Why or why not?

Question 10—Terminology
This Exposure Draft proposes to add to Appendix A of IFRS 17 the definition 'insurance contract services' to be consistent with other proposed amendments in this Exposure Draft. In the light of the proposed amendments in this Exposure Draft, the Board is considering whether to make a consequential change in terminology by amending the terms in IFRS 17 to replace 'coverage' with 'service' in the terms 'coverage units', 'coverage period' and 'liability for remaining coverage'. If that change is made, those terms would become 'service units', 'service period' and 'liability for remaining service', respectively, throughout IFRS 17. Would you find this change in terminology helpful? Why or why not?

How and by when to comment

We would prefer to receive your comments electronically; however, comments can be submitted using any of the following methods:

Electronically	Visit the 'Open for comment' page at: http://go.ifrs.org/open-for-comment
By email	Send email comments to: commentletters@ifrs.org
By post	IFRS Foundation Columbus Building 7 Westferry Circus Canary Wharf London E14 4HD United Kingdom

The Board will consider all comments received in writing by 25 September 2019.

Unless confidentiality is specifically requested, all comments will be posted on our website. Requests for confidentiality will not normally be granted unless supported by a good reason, for example, commercial confidence. Please see our website for details on this policy, and on how we use your personal data.

[Draft] Amendments to IFRS 17 *Insurance Contracts*

Paragraphs 4 and 7 are amended, and paragraph 8A is added. Deleted text is struck through and new text is underlined.

Scope

...

4 All references in IFRS 17 to insurance contracts also apply to:

(a) reinsurance contracts held, except:

(i) ...

(ii) as described in paragraphs 60–70A~~70~~.

(b) ...

...

7 An entity shall not apply IFRS 17 to:

(a) ...

(h) credit card contracts that meet the definition of an insurance contract if, and only if, the entity does not reflect an assessment of the insurance risk associated with an individual customer in setting the price of the contract with that customer (see IFRS 9 *Financial Instruments*).

...

8A Some contracts meet the definition of an insurance contract but limit the compensation for insured events to the amount required to settle the policyholder's obligation created by the contract (for example, loans with death waivers). If such contracts are not excluded from the scope of IFRS 17 by paragraphs 7(a)–(h), an entity shall choose to apply IFRS 17 or IFRS 9 to such contracts that it issues. The entity shall make that choice for each portfolio of insurance contracts, and the choice for each portfolio is irrevocable.

Paragraphs 10–12 are amended. New text is underlined and deleted text is struck through.

Separating components from an insurance contract (paragraphs B31–B35)

10 An insurance contract may contain one or more components that would be within the scope of another Standard if they were separate contracts. For example, an insurance contract may include an *investment component* or a non-insurance service component (or both). An entity shall apply paragraphs 11–13 to identify and account for the components of the contract.

11 An entity shall:

(a) ...

(b) separate from a host insurance contract an investment component if, and only if, that investment component is distinct (see paragraphs B31–B32). The entity shall apply IFRS 9 to account for the separated investment component unless it is an investment contract with discretionary participation features (see paragraph 3(c)).

12 After applying paragraph 11 to separate any cash flows related to embedded derivatives and distinct investment components, an entity shall separate from the host insurance contract any promise to transfer to a policyholder distinct goods or ~~non-insurance~~ services other than *insurance contract services* ~~to a policyholder~~, applying paragraph 7 of IFRS 15. The entity shall account for such promises applying IFRS 15. In applying paragraph 7 of IFRS 15 to separate the promise, the entity shall apply paragraphs B33–B35 of IFRS 17 and, on initial recognition, shall:

(a) apply IFRS 15 to attribute the cash inflows between the insurance component and any promises to provide distinct goods or ~~non-insurance~~ services other than insurance contract services; and

(b) attribute the cash outflows between the insurance component and any promised goods or ~~non-insurance~~ services other than insurance contract services, accounted for applying IFRS 15 so that:

(i) ...

...

Paragraphs 19 and 24 are amended. New text is underlined and deleted text is struck through.

Level of aggregation of insurance contracts

...

19 For contracts issued to which an entity does not apply the premium allocation approach (see paragraphs 53–54~~59~~), an entity shall assess whether contracts that are not onerous at initial recognition have no significant possibility of becoming onerous:

(a) ...

...

24 An entity shall apply the recognition and measurement requirements of IFRS 17 to the groups of contracts ~~issued~~ determined by applying paragraphs 14–23. An entity shall establish the groups at initial recognition and add contracts to the group applying paragraph 28.~~, and~~ The entity shall not reassess the composition of the groups subsequently. To measure a group of contracts, an entity may estimate the *fulfilment cash flows* at a higher level of aggregation than the group or portfolio, provided the entity is able to include the appropriate fulfilment cash flows in the measurement of the group,

applying paragraphs 32(a), 40(a)(i) and 40(b), by allocating such estimates to groups of contracts.

Paragraph 27 is deleted, paragraph 28 is amended and paragraphs 28A–28D are added. Paragraph 25 is not amended, but is included for ease of reference. New text is underlined and deleted text is struck through.

Recognition

25 **An entity shall recognise a group of insurance contracts it issues from the earliest of the following:**

(a) **the beginning of the *coverage period* of the group of contracts;**

(b) **the date when the first payment from a policyholder in the group becomes due; and**

(c) **for a group of onerous contracts, when the group becomes onerous.**

...

27 [Deleted]~~An entity shall recognise an asset or liability for any *insurance acquisition cash flows* relating to a group of issued insurance contracts that the entity pays or receives before the group is recognised, unless it chooses to recognise them as expenses or income applying paragraph 59(a). An entity shall derecognise the asset or liability resulting from such insurance acquisition cash flows when the group of insurance contracts to which the cash flows are allocated is recognised (see paragraph 38(b)).~~

28 In recognising a group of insurance contracts in a reporting period, an entity shall include only contracts that individually meet one of the criteria set out in paragraph 25 ~~issued by the end of the reporting period~~ and shall make estimates for the discount rates at the date of initial recognition (see paragraph B73) and the coverage units provided in the reporting period (see paragraph B119). An entity may include ~~issue~~ more contracts in the group after the end of a reporting period, subject to paragraphs 14–22~~paragraph 22~~. An entity shall add the contracts to the group in the reporting period in which the contracts meet one of the criteria set out in paragraph 25 ~~are issued~~. This may result in a change to the determination of the discount rates at the date of initial recognition applying paragraph B73. An entity shall apply the revised rates from the start of the reporting period in which the new contracts are added to the group.

28A An entity applying the premium allocation approach may recognise insurance acquisition cash flows as expenses applying paragraph 59(a). Otherwise, the entity shall allocate insurance acquisition cash flows to a group of insurance contracts on a systematic and rational basis applying paragraph B35A.

28B An entity shall recognise:

(a) insurance acquisition cash flows it expects to pay after the related group of insurance contracts is recognised as part of the fulfilment cash flows of the group of insurance contracts applying paragraph 32(a).

(b) insurance acquisition cash flows paid before the related group of insurance contracts is recognised as an asset. An entity shall recognise such an asset for each existing or future group of insurance contracts to which insurance acquisition cash flows are allocated.

28C An entity shall derecognise an asset recognised applying paragraph 28B(b) when the insurance acquisition cash flows allocated to the group of insurance contracts are included in the measurement of the group applying paragraph 38(b). If, applying paragraph 28, the entity recognises in a reporting period only some of the insurance contracts expected to be included in the group, the entity shall determine the related portion of an asset for insurance acquisition cash flows for the group on a systematic and rational basis considering the expected timing of recognition of contracts in the group. The entity shall derecognise that portion of the asset and include it in the measurement of a group of insurance contracts applying paragraph 38(b).

28D At the end of each reporting period, an entity shall assess the recoverability of an asset recognised applying paragraph 28B(b) if facts and circumstances indicate the asset may be impaired. If facts and circumstances indicate the asset may be impaired, the entity shall adjust the carrying amount of the asset and recognise any impairment loss identified applying paragraph B35B. An entity shall adjust the carrying amount of the asset and recognise the reversal of any such loss applying paragraph B35C.

Paragraph 29 is amended and its heading is amended. New text is underlined and deleted text is struck through.

Measurement (paragraphs B36–B119FB119)

29 An entity shall apply paragraphs 30–52 to all groups of insurance contracts within the scope of IFRS 17, with the following exceptions:

(a) ...

(b) for groups of reinsurance contracts held, an entity shall apply paragraphs 32–46 as required by paragraphs 63–70A70. Paragraphs 45 (on *insurance contracts with direct participation features*) and paragraphs 47–52 (on onerous contracts) do not apply to groups of reinsurance contracts held.

(c) ...

...

> The heading for paragraph 32 is amended. Paragraph 32 is not amended, but is included for ease of reference. Paragraphs 34 and 38 are amended. New text is underlined and deleted text is struck through.

Measurement on initial recognition (paragraphs B36–B95C~~B95~~)

32 **On initial recognition, an entity shall measure a group of insurance contracts at the total of:**

(a) ...

Estimates of future cash flows (paragraphs B36–B71)

...

34 Cash flows are within the boundary of an insurance contract if they arise from substantive rights and obligations that exist during the reporting period in which the entity can compel the policyholder to pay the premiums or in which the entity has a substantive obligation to provide the policyholder with insurance contract services (see paragraphs B61–B71). A substantive obligation to provide insurance contract services ends when:

(a) ...

(b) both of the following criteria are satisfied:

(i) the entity has the practical ability to reassess the risks of the portfolio of insurance contracts that contains the contract and, as a result, can set a price or level of benefits that fully reflects the risk of that portfolio; and

(ii) the pricing of the premiums ~~for coverage~~ up to the date when the risks are reassessed does not take into account the risks that relate to periods after the reassessment date.

...

Contractual service margin

38 **The contractual service margin is a component of the asset or liability for the group of insurance contracts that represents the unearned profit the entity will recognise as it provides insurance contract services in the future. An entity shall measure the contractual service margin on initial recognition of a group of insurance contracts at an amount that, unless paragraph 47 (on onerous contracts) applies, results in no income or expenses arising from:**

(a) ...

(b) **the derecognition at the date of initial recognition of any asset or liability recognised for insurance acquisition cash flows applying paragraph 28C ~~27~~; and**

(c) ...

...

Paragraphs 41, 44 and 45 are amended and the heading for paragraphs 44 and 45 is amended. New text is underlined and deleted text is struck through.

Subsequent measurement

...

41 **An entity shall recognise income and expenses for the following changes in the carrying amount of the liability for remaining coverage:**

(a) **insurance revenue – for the reduction in the liability for remaining coverage because of insurance contract services provided in the period, measured applying paragraphs B120–B124;**

(b) ...

...

Contractual service margin (paragraphs B96–B119B~~B119~~)

...

44 For *insurance contracts without direct participation features*, the carrying amount of the contractual service margin of a group of contracts at the end of the reporting period equals the carrying amount at the start of the reporting period adjusted for:

(a) ...

(e) the amount recognised as insurance revenue because of the transfer of insurance contract services in the period, determined by the allocation of the contractual service margin remaining at the end of the reporting period (before any allocation) over the current and remaining coverage period applying paragraph B119.

45 For insurance contracts with direct participation features (see paragraphs B101–B118), the carrying amount of the contractual service margin of a group of contracts at the end of the reporting period equals the carrying amount at the start of the reporting period adjusted for the amounts specified in subparagraphs (a)–(e) below. An entity is not required to identify these adjustments separately. Instead, a combined amount may be determined for some, or all, of the adjustments. The adjustments are:

(a) ...

(b) the change in the amount of the entity's share of the ~~change in the~~ fair value of the *underlying items* (see paragraph B104(b)(i)), except to the extent that:

(i) paragraph B115 (on risk mitigation) applies;

(ii) the<u> decrease in the amount of the</u> entity's share of~~ a decrease in~~ the fair value of the underlying items exceeds the carrying amount of the contractual service margin, giving rise to a loss (see paragraph 48); or

(iii) the<u> increase in the amount of the</u> entity's share of~~ an increase in~~ the fair value of the underlying items reverses the amount in (ii).

(c) ...

(e) the amount recognised as insurance revenue because of the transfer of <u>insurance contract</u> services in the period, determined by the allocation of the contractual service margin remaining at the end of the reporting period (before any allocation) over the current and remaining coverage period~~,~~ applying paragraph B119.

...

> Paragraphs 47–48 and 50 are amended. New text is underlined and deleted text is struck through.

Onerous contracts

47 An insurance contract is onerous at the date of initial recognition if the fulfilment cash flows allocated to the contract, any previously recognised <u>insurance</u> acquisition cash flows and any cash flows arising from the contract at the date of initial recognition in total are a net outflow. Applying paragraph 16(a), an entity shall group such contracts separately from contracts that are not onerous. To the extent that paragraph 17 applies, an entity may identify the group of onerous contracts by measuring a set of contracts rather than individual contracts. An entity shall recognise a loss in profit or loss for the net outflow for the group of onerous contracts, resulting in the carrying amount of the liability for the group being equal to the fulfilment cash flows and the contractual service margin of the group being zero.

48 A group of insurance contracts becomes onerous (or more onerous) on subsequent measurement if the following amounts exceed the carrying amount of the contractual service margin:

(a) unfavourable changes<u> relating to future service</u> in the fulfilment cash flows allocated to the group~~,~~ arising from changes in estimates of future cash flows<u> and the risk adjustment for non-financial risk</u> ~~relating to future service~~; and

(b) for a group of insurance contracts with direct participation features, the<u> decrease in the amount of the</u> entity's share of~~ a decrease in~~ the fair value of the underlying items.

Applying paragraphs 44(c)(i), 45(b)(ii) and 45(c)(ii), an entity shall recognise a loss in profit or loss to the extent of that excess.

...

50 After an entity has recognised a loss on an onerous group of insurance contracts, it shall allocate:

(a) ...

(b) solely to the loss component until that component is reduced to zero:

(i) any subsequent decrease relating to future service in fulfilment cash flows allocated to the group arising from changes in estimates of future cash flows and the risk adjustment for non-financial risk; ~~relating to future service~~ and

(ii) any subsequent increases in the amount of the entity's share of ~~in~~ the fair value of the underlying items ~~solely to the loss component until that component is reduced to zero~~.

Applying paragraphs 44(c)(ii), 45(b)(iii) and 45(c)(iii), an entity shall adjust the contractual service margin only for the excess of the decrease over the amount allocated to the loss component.

...

Paragraphs 53 and 55–56 are amended. New text is underlined and deleted text is struck through.

Premium allocation approach

53 An entity may simplify the measurement of a group of insurance contracts using the premium allocation approach set out in paragraphs 55–59 if, and only if, at the inception of the group:

(a) the entity reasonably expects that such simplification would produce a measurement of the liability for remaining coverage for the group that would not differ materially from the one that would be produced applying the requirements in paragraphs 32–52; or

(b) the coverage period of each contract in the group (including insurance contract services ~~coverage~~ arising from all premiums within the contract boundary determined at that date applying paragraph 34) is one year or less.

...

55 Using the premium allocation approach, an entity shall measure the liability for remaining coverage as follows:

(a) on initial recognition, the carrying amount of the liability is:

(i) ...

(iii) plus or minus any amount arising from the derecognition at that date of the asset ~~or liability~~ recognised for insurance acquisition cash flows applying paragraph 28C ~~27~~.

(b) at the end of each subsequent reporting period, the carrying amount of the liability is the carrying amount at the start of the reporting period:

(i) ...

(v) minus the amount recognised as insurance revenue for insurance contract services ~~coverage~~ provided in that period (see paragraph B126); and

(vi) ...

56 If insurance contracts in the group have a significant financing component, an entity shall adjust the carrying amount of the liability for remaining coverage to reflect the time value of money and the effect of financial risk using the discount rates specified in paragraph 36, as determined on initial recognition. The entity is not required to adjust the carrying amount of the liability for remaining coverage to reflect the time value of money and the effect of financial risk if, at initial recognition, the entity expects that the time between providing each part of the insurance contract services ~~coverage~~ and the related premium due date is no more than a year.

...

Paragraphs 60, 62, 65–66 and 69 are amended, paragraph 65 is bifurcated creating new paragraph 65A, paragraphs 66A–66B and 70A are added. New text is underlined and deleted text is struck through.

Reinsurance contracts held

60 The requirements in IFRS 17 are modified for reinsurance contracts held, as set out in paragraphs 61–70A~~70~~.

...

Recognition

62 Instead of applying paragraph 25, an entity shall recognise ~~a group of reinsurance contracts held~~:

(a) a group of *reinsurance contracts held that provide proportionate coverage*: ~~if the reinsurance contracts held provide proportionate coverage~~

(i) unless paragraph 62(a)(ii) applies—at the beginning of the coverage period of the group of reinsurance contracts held or at the initial recognition of any underlying contract, whichever is the later; or ~~and~~

(ii) if the entity recognises an onerous group of underlying contracts before the beginning of the coverage period of the group of reinsurance contracts held—at the same time as the onerous group of underlying contracts.

(b) ~~in~~ all other groups of reinsurance contracts held ~~cases~~—from the beginning of the coverage period of the group of reinsurance contracts held.

Measurement

...

65 The requirements of paragraph 38 that relate to determining the contractual service margin on initial recognition are modified to reflect the fact that for a group of reinsurance contracts held there is no unearned profit but instead a net cost or net gain on purchasing the reinsurance. Hence, unless paragraph 65A applies, on initial recognition~~: (a)~~ the entity shall recognise any net cost or net gain on purchasing the group of reinsurance contracts held as a contractual service margin measured at an amount equal to the sum of:

(a) the fulfilment cash flows;~~,~~

(b) the amount derecognised at that date of any asset or liability previously recognised for cash flows related to the group of reinsurance contracts held;~~, and~~

(c) any cash flows arising at that date; and

(d) any income recognised in profit or loss applying paragraph 66A.~~; unless~~

65A If ~~(b)~~ the net cost of purchasing reinsurance coverage relates to events that occurred before the purchase of the group of reinsurance contracts,~~ in which case,~~ notwithstanding the requirements of paragraph B5, the entity shall recognise such a cost immediately in profit or loss as an expense.

66 Instead of applying paragraph 44, an entity shall measure the contractual service margin at the end of the reporting period for a group of reinsurance contracts held as the carrying amount determined at the start of the reporting period, adjusted for:

(a) ...

(ba) income recognised in profit or loss in the reporting period applying paragraph 66A;

(c) ...

66A An entity shall adjust the contractual service margin of a group of reinsurance contracts held that provides proportionate coverage and as a result recognise income when the entity recognises a loss on initial recognition of an onerous group of underlying insurance contracts or on addition of onerous underlying insurance contracts to that group. The amount of the adjustment and resulting income is determined applying paragraph B119D.

66B An entity shall establish (or adjust) a loss-recovery component of the asset for remaining coverage for a group of reinsurance contracts held depicting the recovery of losses recognised applying paragraph 66A (see paragraphs B119E–B119F).

...

Premium allocation approach for reinsurance contracts held

69 An entity may use the premium allocation approach set out in paragraphs 55–56 and 59 (adapted to reflect the features of reinsurance contracts held that differ from insurance contracts issued, for example the generation of expenses or reduction in expenses rather than revenue) to simplify the measurement of a group of reinsurance contracts held, if at the inception of the group:

(a) the entity reasonably expects the resulting measurement would not differ materially from the result of applying the requirements in paragraphs 63–68; or

(b) the coverage period of each contract in the group of reinsurance contracts held (including <u>insurance</u> coverage from all premiums within the contract boundary determined at that date applying paragraph 34) is one year or less.

...

<u>70A</u> <u>An entity shall apply paragraph 66A when a group of reinsurance contracts held is accounted for applying the premium allocation approach, by adjusting the carrying amount of the asset for remaining coverage instead of adjusting the contractual service margin.</u>

Paragraph 71 is amended. New text is underlined and deleted text is struck through.

Investment contracts with discretionary participation features

71 An investment contract with discretionary participation features does not include a transfer of significant insurance risk. Consequently, the requirements in IFRS 17 for insurance contracts are modified for investment contracts with discretionary participation features as follows:

(a) the date of initial recognition (see <u>paragraphs 25 and 28</u>~~paragraph 25~~) is the date the entity becomes party to the contract.

(b) ...

...

Paragraph 76 is amended. New text is underlined and deleted text is struck through.

Modification and derecognition

...

Derecognition

...

76 An entity derecognises an insurance contract from within a group of contracts by applying the following requirements in IFRS 17:

(a) ...

(c) the number of coverage units for expected remaining <u>insurance contract services</u> ~~coverage~~ is adjusted to reflect the coverage units derecognised from the group, and the amount of the contractual service margin recognised in profit or loss in the period is based on that adjusted number~~,~~ applying paragraph B119.

...

Paragraphs 78–79 are amended. New text is underlined and deleted text is struck through.

Presentation in the statement of financial position

78 **An entity shall present separately in the statement of financial position the carrying amount of <u>portfolios</u> ~~groups~~ of:**

(a) insurance contracts issued that are assets;

(b) insurance contracts issued that are liabilities;

(c) reinsurance contracts held that are assets; and

(d) reinsurance contracts held that are liabilities.

79 An entity shall include any assets ~~or liabilities~~ for insurance acquisition cash flows recognised applying paragraph <u>28B(b)</u> ~~27~~ in the carrying amount of the related <u>portfolios</u> ~~groups~~ of insurance contracts issued, and any assets or liabilities for cash flows related to <u>portfolios</u> ~~groups~~ of reinsurance contracts held (see paragraph 65(a)) in the carrying amount of the <u>portfolios</u> ~~groups~~ of reinsurance contracts held.

Paragraphs 83 and 86 are amended. New text is underlined and deleted text is struck through.

Recognition and presentation in the statement(s) of financial performance (paragraphs B120–B136)

...

Insurance service result

83 **An entity shall present in profit or loss insurance revenue arising from the groups of insurance contracts issued. Insurance revenue shall depict the provision of <u>insurance contract services</u> ~~coverage and other services~~ arising from the group of insurance contracts at an amount that reflects the consideration to which the entity expects to be entitled in exchange for those services. Paragraphs B120–B127 specify how an entity measures insurance revenue.**

...

86 An entity may present the income or expenses from a group of reinsurance contracts held (see paragraphs 60–70A~~70~~), other than insurance finance income or expenses, as a single amount; or the entity may present separately the amounts recovered from the reinsurer and an allocation of the premiums paid that together give a net amount equal to that single amount. If an entity presents separately the amounts recovered from the reinsurer and an allocation of the premiums paid, it shall:

(a) treat reinsurance cash flows that are contingent on claims on the underlying contracts as part of the claims that are expected to be reimbursed under the reinsurance contract held;

(b) treat amounts from the reinsurer that it expects to receive that are not contingent on claims of the underlying contracts (for example, some types of ceding commissions) as a reduction in the premiums to be paid to the reinsurer;~~ and~~

(c) not present the allocation of premiums paid as a reduction in revenue; and~~.~~

(d) treat amounts recognised relating to recovery of losses applying paragraphs 66A–66B as amounts recovered from the reinsurer (see paragraphs B119E–B119F).

...

Disclosure

...

Paragraphs 97, 99–101, 103–105, 106 and 109 are amended, paragraphs 105A–105C are added. Paragraph 98 is not amended, but is included for ease of reference. New text is underlined and deleted text is struck through.

Explanation of recognised amounts

97 Of the disclosures required by paragraphs 98–109, only those in paragraphs 98–100~~, and~~ 102–103 and 105–105C apply to contracts to which the premium allocation approach has been applied. If an entity uses the premium allocation approach, it shall also disclose:

(a) ...

(b) whether it makes an adjustment for the time value of money and the effect of financial risk applying paragraphs 56 and~~,~~ 57(b)~~ and 59(b)~~; and

(c) ...

98 An entity shall disclose reconciliations that show how the net carrying amounts of contracts within the scope of IFRS 17 changed during the period because of cash flows and income and expenses recognised in the statement(s) of financial performance. Separate reconciliations shall be disclosed for insurance contracts issued and reinsurance contracts held. An entity shall adapt the requirements of paragraphs 100–109 to reflect the features of

reinsurance contracts held that differ from insurance contracts issued; for example, the generation of expenses or reduction in expenses rather than revenue.

99 An entity shall provide enough information in the reconciliations to enable users of financial statements to identify changes from cash flows and amounts that are recognised in the statement(s) of financial performance. To comply with this requirement, an entity shall:

(a) disclose, in a table, the reconciliations set out in paragraphs 100–105C~~105~~; and

(b) for each reconciliation, present the net carrying amounts at the beginning and at the end of the period, disaggregated into a total for portfolios ~~groups~~ of contracts that are assets and a total for portfolios ~~groups~~ of contracts that are liabilities, that equal the amounts presented in the statement of financial position applying paragraph 78.

100 An entity shall disclose reconciliations from the opening to the closing balances separately for each of:

(a) ...

(c) the liabilities for incurred claims. For insurance contracts to which the premium allocation approach described in paragraphs 53–59 or 69–70A~~70~~ has been applied, an entity shall disclose separate reconciliations for:

(i) ...

101 For insurance contracts other than those to which the premium allocation approach described in paragraphs 53–59 or 69–70A~~70~~ has been applied, an entity shall also disclose reconciliations from the opening to the closing balances separately for each of:

(a) ...

...

103 An entity shall separately disclose in the reconciliations required in paragraph 100 each of the following amounts related to insurance contract services, if applicable:

(a) ...

(c) investment components (combined with refunds of premiums unless refunds of premiums are presented as part of the cash flows in the period described in paragraph 105(a)(i)) excluded from insurance revenue and insurance service expenses.

104 An entity shall separately disclose in the reconciliations required in paragraph 101 each of the following amounts related to insurance contract services, if applicable:

(a) ...

(b) changes that relate to current service, ie:

(i) ...

(ii) the change in the risk adjustment for non-financial risk that does not relate to future service or past service; and

(iii) *experience adjustments* (see paragraphs B97(c) and B113(a)), excluding amounts relating to the risk adjustment for non-financial risk included in (ii).

(c) ...

105 To complete the reconciliations in paragraphs 100–101, an entity shall also disclose separately each of the following amounts not related to insurance contract services provided in the period, if applicable:

(a) ...

105A An entity shall disclose a reconciliation from the opening to the closing balance of assets for insurance acquisition cash flows recognised applying paragraphs 28B(b). An entity shall aggregate information for the reconciliation at a level that is consistent with that for the reconciliation of insurance contracts, applying paragraph 98.

105B An entity shall disclose quantitatively, in appropriate time bands, when it expects to derecognise an asset for insurance acquisition cash flows applying paragraph 28C and include those cash flows in the measurement of the group of insurance contracts to which they are allocated.

105C An entity shall separately disclose in the reconciliation required by paragraph 105A any recognition of impairment losses and reversals of impairment losses applying paragraph 28D.

106 For insurance contracts issued other than those to which the premium allocation approach described in paragraphs 53–59 has been applied, an entity shall disclose an analysis of the insurance revenue recognised in the period comprising:

(a) the amounts relating to the changes in the liability for remaining coverage as specified in paragraph B124, separately disclosing:

(i) the insurance service expenses incurred during the period as specified in paragraph B124(a);

(ii) the change in the risk adjustment for non-financial risk, as specified in paragraph B124(b); ~~and~~

(iii) the amount of the contractual service margin recognised in profit or loss because of the transfer of insurance contract services in the period, as specified in paragraph B124(c); and~~.~~

(iv) experience adjustments for premium receipts, if any, as specified in paragraph B124(d).

(b) the allocation of the portion of the premiums that relate to the recovery of insurance acquisition cash flows (see paragraph B125).

...

109 For insurance contracts other than those to which the premium allocation approach described in paragraphs 53–59 or 69–70A~~70~~ has been applied, an entity shall disclose~~ an explanation of~~ when it expects to recognise the contractual service margin remaining at the end of the reporting period in profit or loss~~, either~~ quantitatively, in appropriate time bands~~, or by providing qualitative information~~. Such information shall be provided separately for insurance contracts issued and reinsurance contracts held.

Paragraph 117 is amended. New text is underlined and deleted text is struck through.

Significant judgements in applying IFRS 17

117 An entity shall disclose the significant judgements and changes in judgements made in applying IFRS 17. Specifically, an entity shall disclose the inputs, assumptions and estimation techniques used, including:

(a) ...

(c) to the extent not covered in (a), the approach used:

(i) ...

(iii) to determine discount rates;~~ and~~

(iv) to determine investment components; and~~.~~

(v) to determine the relative weighting of the benefits provided by insurance coverage and investment-return service (for insurance contracts without direct participation features) or insurance coverage and investment-related service (for insurance contracts with direct participation features) (see paragraphs B119–B119B).

...

Paragraphs 128–129 and 132 are amended. New text is underlined and deleted text is struck through.

Nature and extent of risks that arise from contracts within the scope of IFRS 17

...

Insurance and market risks—sensitivity analysis

128 An entity shall disclose information about sensitivities to changes in risk variables~~ exposures~~ arising from contracts within the scope of IFRS 17. To comply with this requirement, an entity shall disclose:

(a) a sensitivity analysis that shows how profit or loss and equity would have been affected by changes in risk variables~~ exposures~~ that were reasonably possible at the end of the reporting period:

(i) ...

(ii) for each type of market risk—in a way that explains the relationship between the sensitivities to changes in risk variables ~~exposures~~ arising from insurance contracts and those arising from financial assets held by the entity.

(b) ...

129 If an entity prepares a sensitivity analysis that shows how amounts different from those specified in paragraph 128(a) are affected by changes in risk variables ~~exposures~~ and uses that sensitivity analysis to manage risks arising from contracts within the scope of IFRS 17, it may use that sensitivity analysis in place of the analysis specified in paragraph 128(a). The entity shall also disclose:

(a) ...

...

Liquidity risk—other information

132 For liquidity risk arising from contracts within the scope of IFRS 17, an entity shall disclose:

(a) a description of how it manages the liquidity risk.

(b) separate maturity analyses for portfolios ~~groups~~ of insurance contracts issued that are liabilities and portfolios ~~groups~~ of reinsurance contracts held that are liabilities that show, as a minimum, net cash flows of the portfolios ~~groups~~ for each of the first five years after the reporting date and in aggregate beyond the first five years. An entity is not required to include in these analyses liabilities for remaining coverage measured applying paragraphs 55–59 and paragraphs 69–70A. The analyses may take the form of:

(i) an analysis, by estimated timing, of the remaining contractual undiscounted net cash flows; or

(ii) an analysis, by estimated timing, of the estimates of the present value of the future cash flows.

(c) the amounts that are payable on demand, explaining the relationship between such amounts and the carrying amount of the related portfolios ~~groups~~ of contracts, if not disclosed applying (b) of this paragraph.

[Draft] Amendments to Appendix A—Defined terms

The definitions of 'contractual service margin', 'coverage period', 'group of insurance contracts' and 'insurance acquisition cash flows' are amended. New text is underlined and deleted text is struck through.

contractual service margin	A component of the carrying amount of the asset or liability for a **group of insurance contracts** representing the unearned profit the entity will recognise as it provides **insurance contract services** ~~**services**~~ under the **insurance contracts** in the group.
coverage period	The period during which the entity provides **insurance contract services** ~~**coverage for insured events**~~. This period includes the services ~~**coverage**~~ that relates to all premiums within the boundary of the **insurance contract**.
…	
group of insurance contracts	A set of **insurance contracts** resulting from the division of a **portfolio of insurance contracts** into, at a minimum, contracts issued or expected to be issued ~~**written**~~ within a period of no longer than one year and that, at initial recognition: (a) are onerous, if any; (b) have no significant possibility of becoming onerous subsequently, if any; or (c) do not fall into either (a) or (b), if any.
insurance acquisition cash flows	Cash flows arising from the costs of selling, underwriting and starting a **group of insurance contracts** (issued or expected to be issued) that are directly attributable to the **portfolio of insurance contracts** to which the group belongs. Such cash flows include cash flows that are not directly attributable to individual contracts or **groups of insurance contracts** within the portfolio.

A new definition is added after the definition of 'insurance contract'. New text is underlined.

insurance contract services	The following services that an entity provides to a policyholder of an insurance contract: (a) coverage for an **insured event** (insurance coverage); (b) for insurance contracts without direct participation features, the generation of an investment return for the policyholder, if applicable (investment-return service); and

(c) for insurance contracts with direct participation features, the management of underlying items on behalf of the policyholder (investment-related service).

The definitions of 'investment component', 'liability for incurred claims' and 'liability for remaining coverage' are amended. New text is underlined and deleted text is struck through.

investment component — The amounts that an **insurance contract** requires the entity to repay to a **policyholder** in all circumstances, regardless of whether an insured event occurs ~~even if an **insured event** does not occur~~.

...

liability for incurred claims — An entity's obligation to:

(a) investigate and pay valid claims for **insured events** that have already occurred, including events that have occurred but for which claims have not been reported, and other incurred insurance expenses; and~~.~~

(b) pay amounts under existing insurance contracts that are not included in (a) for which an entity no longer provides an investment-return service or an investment-related service.

liability for remaining coverage — An entity's obligation to:

(a) investigate and pay valid claims under existing **insurance contracts** for **insured events** that have not yet occurred (ie the obligation that relates to the unexpired portion of the insurance coverage ~~**coverage period**~~); and~~.~~

(b) pay amounts under existing contracts that are not included in (a) for which an entity will provide an investment-return service or an investment-related service.

A new definition is added after the definition of 'reinsurance contract'. New text is underlined.

reinsurance contract held that provides proportionate coverage — A reinsurance contract held that provides an entity with the right to recover from the issuer a percentage of all claims incurred on groups of underlying insurance contracts. The percentage the entity has a right to recover is fixed for all contracts in a single group of underlying insurance contracts, but can vary between groups of underlying insurance contracts.

[Draft] Amendments to Appendix B—Application guidance

Paragraph B1 is amended. New text is underlined.

B1 This appendix provides guidance on the following:

(a) ...

(ba) asset for insurance acquisition cash flows (see paragraphs B35A–B35C);

(c) measurement (see paragraphs B36–B119F~~B119~~);

(d) ...

Paragraphs B5 and B12 are amended. New text is underlined.

Definition of an insurance contract (Appendix A)

...

Uncertain future event

...

B5 Some insurance contracts cover events that have already occurred but the financial effect of which is still uncertain. An example is an insurance contract that provides insurance coverage against an adverse development of an event that has already occurred. In such contracts, the insured event is the determination of the ultimate cost of those claims.

...

The distinction between insurance risk and other risks

...

B12 The definition of an insurance contract refers to an adverse effect on the policyholder. This definition does not limit the payment by the entity to an amount equal to the financial effect of the adverse event. For example, the definition includes 'new for old' insurance coverage that pays the policyholder an amount that permits the replacement of a used and damaged asset with a new one. Similarly, the definition does not limit the payment under a life insurance contract to the financial loss suffered by the deceased's dependants, nor does it exclude contracts that specify the payment of predetermined amounts to quantify the loss caused by death or an accident.

...

After paragraph B35, a new heading and paragraphs B35A–B35C are added. New text is underlined.

Asset for insurance acquisition cash flows (paragraphs 28A–28D)

B35A To apply paragraph 28A, an entity allocates insurance acquisition cash flows that are directly attributable to a group of insurance contracts:

(a) to that group; and

(b) to groups that include insurance contracts that are expected to arise from renewal of the insurance contracts in that group.

B35B To apply paragraph 28D:

(a) an entity shall recognise an impairment loss in profit or loss and reduce the carrying amount of any asset for insurance acquisition cash flows recognised applying paragraph 28B(b), so that the carrying amount of each asset does not exceed the expected net cash inflow for the related group, determined applying paragraph 32(a).

(b) in addition, when an entity allocates insurance acquisition cash flows to groups of insurance contracts applying paragraph B35A(b), the entity shall recognise an impairment loss in profit or loss and reduce the carrying amount of the related assets for insurance acquisition cash flows to the extent that:

(i) the entity expects those insurance acquisition cash flows to exceed the net cash inflow for the expected renewals, determined applying paragraph 32(a); and

(ii) the excess determined applying paragraph B35B(b)(i) has not already been recognised as an impairment loss applying paragraph B35B(a).

B35C An entity shall recognise in profit or loss a reversal of some or all of an impairment loss previously recognised applying paragraph 28D and increase the carrying amount of the asset, to the extent that the impairment conditions no longer exist or have improved.

Paragraphs B64–B65 and B71 are amended. New text is underlined and deleted text is struck through.

Measurement (paragraphs 29–71)

Estimates of future cash flows (paragraphs 33–35)

...

Cash flows within the contract boundary (paragraph 34)

...

B64 Paragraph 34 refers to an entity's practical ability to set a price at a future date (a renewal date) that fully reflects the risks in the contract from that date. An entity has that practical ability in the absence of constraints that prevent the entity from setting the same price it would for a new contract with the same characteristics as the existing contract issued on that date, or if it can amend the benefits to be consistent with the price it will charge. Similarly, an entity has that practical ability to set a price when it can reprice an existing contract so that the price reflects overall changes in the risks in a portfolio of insurance contracts, even if the price set for each individual policyholder does not reflect the change in risk for that specific policyholder. When assessing whether the entity has the practical ability to set a price that fully reflects the risks in the contract or portfolio, it shall consider all the risks that it would consider when underwriting equivalent contracts on the renewal date for the remaining service ~~coverage~~. In determining the estimates of future cash flows at the end of a reporting period, an entity shall reassess the boundary of an insurance contract to include the effect of changes in circumstances on the entity's substantive rights and obligations.

B65 Cash flows within the boundary of an insurance contract are those that relate directly to the fulfilment of the contract, including cash flows for which the entity has discretion over the amount or timing. The cash flows within the boundary include:

(a) ...

(la) costs the entity will incur in providing an investment-return service (for insurance contracts without direct participation features) or an investment-related service (for insurance contracts with direct participation features).

(m) ...

...

Contracts with cash flows that affect or are affected by cash flows to policyholders of other contracts

...

B71 After all the service ~~coverage~~ has been provided to the contracts in a group, the fulfilment cash flows may still include payments expected to be made to current policyholders in other groups or future policyholders. An entity is not required to continue to allocate such fulfilment cash flows to specific groups but can instead recognise and measure a liability for such fulfilment cash flows arising from all groups.

Paragraphs B93–B94 are amended, paragraph B95 is bifurcated creating new paragraph B95A, paragraphs B95B–B95C are added. New text is underlined.

Initial recognition of transfers of insurance contracts and business combinations (paragraph 39)

B93 When an entity acquires insurance contracts issued or reinsurance contracts held in a transfer of insurance contracts that do not form a business or in a business combination within the scope of IFRS 3, the entity shall apply paragraphs 14–24 to identify the groups of contracts acquired, as if it had entered into the contracts on the date of the transaction.

B94 An entity shall use the consideration received or paid for the contracts as a proxy for the premiums received. The consideration received or paid for the contracts excludes the consideration received or paid for any other assets and liabilities acquired in the same transaction. In a business combination within the scope of IFRS 3, the consideration received or paid is the fair value of the contracts at that date. In determining that fair value, an entity shall not apply paragraph 47 of IFRS 13 (relating to demand features).

B95 Unless the premium allocation approach for the liability for remaining coverage in paragraphs 55–59 applies, on initial recognition the contractual service margin is calculated applying paragraph 38 for acquired insurance contracts issued and paragraph 65 for acquired reinsurance contracts held using the consideration received or paid for the contracts as a proxy for the premiums received or paid at the date of initial recognition.

B95A If acquired insurance contracts issued are onerous, applying paragraph 47, the entity shall recognise the excess of the fulfilment cash flows over the consideration paid or received as part of goodwill or gain on a bargain purchase for contracts acquired in a business combination within the scope of IFRS 3 or as a loss in profit or loss for contracts acquired in a transfer. The entity shall establish a loss component of the liability for remaining coverage for that excess, and apply paragraphs 49–52 to allocate subsequent changes in fulfilment cash flows to that loss component.

B95B For a group of reinsurance contracts held to which paragraphs 66A–66B apply at the date of the transaction, an entity shall determine the loss-recovery component of the asset for remaining coverage by multiplying:

(a) the loss component of the liability for remaining coverage of the group of underlying insurance contracts at the date of the transaction; and

(b) the fixed percentage of claims the entity has a right to recover from the group of reinsurance contracts held.

B95C The entity shall recognise the amount of the loss-recovery component determined applying paragraph B95B as part of goodwill or gain on a bargain purchase for reinsurance contracts held acquired in a business combination within the scope of IFRS 3, or as income in profit or loss for contracts acquired in a transfer.

Paragraphs B96–B97 are amended. New text is underlined.

Changes in the carrying amount of the contractual service margin for insurance contracts without direct participation features (paragraph 44)

B96 For insurance contracts without direct participation features, paragraph 44(c) requires an adjustment to the contractual service margin of a group of insurance contracts for changes in fulfilment cash flows that relate to future service. These changes comprise:

(a) experience adjustments arising from premiums received in the period that relate to future service, and related cash flows such as insurance acquisition cash flows and premium-based taxes, measured at the discount rates specified in paragraph B72(c).~~;~~

(b) changes in estimates of the present value of the future cash flows in the liability for remaining coverage, except those described in paragraph B97(a), measured at the discount rates specified in paragraph B72(c).~~;~~

(c) differences between any investment component expected to become payable in the period and the actual investment component that becomes payable in the period, except those described in paragraph B97(a), measured at the discount rates specified in paragraph B72(c).~~;~~ ~~and~~

(d) changes in the risk adjustment for non-financial risk that relate to future service. An entity is not required to disaggregate the change in the risk adjustment for non-financial risk between (i) a change related to non-financial risk and (ii) the effect of the time value of money and changes in the time value of money. If an entity makes such a disaggregation, it shall adjust the contractual service margin for the change related to non-financial risk, measured at the discount rates specified in paragraph B72(c).

B97 An entity shall not adjust the contractual service margin for a group of insurance contracts without direct participation features for the following changes in fulfilment cash flows because they do not relate to future service:

(a) the effect of the time value of money and changes in the time value of money and the effect of financial risk and changes in financial risk (being (i) the effect, if any, on estimated future cash flows; (ii) if the effect is disaggregated, on the risk adjustment for non-financial risk; and (iii) the effect of a change in discount rate);

(b) ...

...

Paragraphs B104, B107, B112, B115, B116 and B118 are amended. Paragraph B101 is not amended, but is included for ease of reference. New text is underlined and deleted text is struck through.

Changes in the carrying amount of the contractual service margin for insurance contracts with direct participation features (paragraph 45)

B101 Insurance contracts with direct participation features are insurance contracts that are substantially investment-related service contracts under which an entity promises an investment return based on underlying items. Hence, they are defined as insurance contracts for which:

(a) the contractual terms specify that the policyholder participates in a share of a clearly identified pool of underlying items (see paragraphs B105–B106);

(b) the entity expects to pay to the policyholder an amount equal to a substantial share of the fair value returns on the underlying items (see paragraph B107); and

(c) the entity expects a substantial proportion of any change in the amounts to be paid to the policyholder to vary with the change in fair value of the underlying items (see paragraph B107).

...

B104 The conditions in paragraph B101 ensure that insurance contracts with direct participation features are contracts under which the entity's obligation to the policyholder is the net of:

(a) ...

(b) a variable fee (see paragraphs B110–B118) that the entity will deduct from (a) in exchange for the future service provided by the insurance contract, comprising:

(i) the amount of the entity's share of the fair value of the underlying items; less

(ii) ...

...

B107 Paragraph B101(b) requires that the entity expects a substantial share of the fair value returns on the underlying items will be paid to the policyholder and paragraph B101(c) requires that the entity expects a substantial proportion of any change in the amounts to be paid to the policyholder to vary with the change in fair value of the underlying items. An entity shall:

(a) ...

(b) assess the variability in the amounts in paragraphs B101(b) and B101(c):

(i) over the duration of the ~~group of~~ insurance contract ~~contracts~~; and

(ii) ...

...

B112 Changes in the amount of the entity's share of the fair value of the underlying items (paragraph B104(b)(i)) relate to future service and adjust the contractual service margin, applying paragraph 45(b).

...

Risk mitigation

B115 To the extent that an entity meets the conditions in paragraph B116, it may choose not to recognise a change in the contractual service margin to reflect some or all of the changes in the effect of financial risk on the amount of the entity's share of the underlying items (see paragraph B112) or the fulfilment cash flows set out in paragraph B113(b).

B116 To apply paragraph B115, an entity must have a previously documented risk-management objective and strategy for mitigating financial risk arising from the insurance contracts using derivatives or reinsurance contracts held, and ~~to mitigate financial risk arising from the insurance contracts and,~~ in applying that objective and strategy:

(a) the entity mitigates the financial risk arising from the insurance contracts using ~~uses~~ a derivative or a reinsurance contract held ~~to mitigate the financial risk arising from the insurance contracts~~.

(b) an economic offset exists between the insurance contracts and the derivative or reinsurance contract held, ie the values of the insurance contracts and the derivative or reinsurance contract held generally move in opposite directions because they respond in a similar way to the changes in the risk being mitigated. An entity shall not consider accounting measurement differences in assessing the economic offset.

(c) credit risk does not dominate the economic offset.

...

B118 If, and only if, any of the conditions in paragraph B116 ceases to be met, an entity shall~~:~~

~~(a)~~ cease to apply paragraph B115 from that date.~~; and~~

~~(b)~~ An entity shall not make any adjustment for changes previously recognised in profit or loss.

Paragraph B119 is amended and paragraphs B119A–B119B are added. New text is underlined and deleted text is struck through.

Recognition of the contractual service margin in profit or loss

B119 An amount of the contractual service margin for a group of insurance contracts is recognised in profit or loss in each period to reflect the insurance contract services provided under the group of insurance contracts in that period (see paragraphs 44(e), 45(e) and 66(e)). The amount is determined by:

(a) identifying the coverage units in the group. The number of coverage units in a group is the quantity of service ~~coverage~~ provided by the contracts in the group, determined by considering for each contract the quantity of the benefits provided under a contract and its expected coverage period ~~duration~~.

(b) allocating the contractual service margin at the end of the period (before recognising any amounts in profit or loss to reflect the insurance contract services provided in the period) equally to each coverage unit provided in the current period and expected to be provided in the future.

(c) recognising in profit or loss the amount allocated to coverage units provided in the period.

B119A For the purpose of applying paragraph B119, the period of investment-return service or investment-related service ends at or before the date that all amounts due to current policyholders relating to those services have been paid, without considering payments to future policyholders included in the fulfilment cash flows applying paragraph B68.

B119B Insurance contracts without direct participation features may provide an investment-return service if, and only if:

(a) an investment component exists, or the policyholder has a right to withdraw an amount;

(b) the entity expects the investment component or amount the policyholder has a right to withdraw to include a positive investment return (a positive investment return could be below zero, for example, in a negative interest rate environment); and

(c) the entity expects to perform investment activity to generate that positive investment return.

A new heading and paragraphs B119C–B119F are added. New text is underlined and deleted text is struck through.

Reinsurance contracts held—recognition of recovery of losses on underlying insurance contracts (paragraphs 66A–66B)

B119C Paragraph 66A applies to reinsurance contracts held that provide proportionate coverage. Such reinsurance contracts provide the entity with the right to recover from the issuer a fixed percentage of all claims incurred on a group of underlying insurance contracts. Such reinsurance contracts can also include cash flows, other than claims, that are not proportionate to cash flows of the underlying groups of insurance contracts issued. For example, in such reinsurance contracts, the premiums due to the reinsurer might not be proportionate to premiums due from the policyholders of the groups of underlying insurance contracts.

B119D An entity shall determine the adjustment to the contractual service margin and the resulting income recognised applying paragraph 66A by multiplying:

(a) the loss recognised on the group of underlying insurance contracts; and

(b) the fixed percentage of claims on the group of underlying insurance contracts the entity has a right to recover from the group of reinsurance contracts held.

B119E Applying paragraph 66B, an entity shall establish (or adjust) a loss-recovery component of the asset for remaining coverage for a group of reinsurance contracts held. The loss-recovery component determines the amounts that are presented in profit or loss as reversals of recoveries of losses from reinsurance contracts held and are consequently excluded from the allocation of premiums paid to the reinsurer.

B119F After an entity has established a loss-recovery component applying paragraph 66B it shall:

(a) adjust the loss-recovery component to reflect changes in the loss component for the group of underlying insurance contracts recognised applying paragraphs 50(a) and 51–52; and

(b) allocate subsequent changes in fulfilment cash flows described in paragraph 66(c)(ii), which arise from onerous groups of underlying insurance contracts, to that loss-recovery component until it is reduced to zero.

Paragraphs B121, B123–B124 and B126 are amended. New text is underlined and deleted text is struck through.

Insurance revenue (paragraphs 83 and 85)

...

B121 Paragraph 83 requires the amount of insurance revenue recognised in a period to depict the transfer of promised services at an amount that reflects the consideration to which the entity expects to be entitled in exchange for those services. The total consideration for a group of contracts covers the following amounts:

(a) amounts related to the provision of services, comprising:

(i) insurance service expenses, excluding any amounts relating to the risk adjustment for non-financial risk included in (ii) and any amounts allocated to the loss component of the liability for remaining coverage;

(ii) the risk adjustment for non-financial risk, excluding any amounts allocated to the loss component of the liability for remaining coverage; and

(iii) ...

...

B123 Applying IFRS 15, when an entity provides services, it derecognises the performance obligation for those services and recognises revenue. Consistently, applying IFRS 17, when an entity provides services in a period, it reduces the liability for remaining coverage for the services provided and recognises insurance revenue. The reduction in the liability for remaining coverage that gives rise to insurance revenue excludes changes in the liability that do not relate to services expected to be covered by the consideration received by the entity. Those changes are:

(a) changes that do not relate to services provided in the period, for example:

(i) ...

(iia) changes resulting from cash flows from loans to policyholders;

(iii) ...

B124 Consequently, insurance revenue for the period can also be analysed as the total of the changes in the liability for remaining coverage in the period that relates to services for which the entity expects to receive consideration. Those changes are:

(a) insurance service expenses incurred in the period (measured at the amounts expected at the beginning of the period), excluding:

(i) ...

(iii) amounts that relate to transaction-based taxes collected on behalf of third parties (such as premium taxes, value added taxes and goods and services taxes) (see paragraph B65(i));~~ and~~

(iv) insurance acquisition expenses (see paragraph B125); and~~.~~

(v) the amount related to the risk adjustment for non-financial risk (see (b)).

(b) ...

(c) ...

(d) experience adjustments for premium receipts, if any.

...

B126 When an entity applies the premium allocation approach in paragraphs 55–58, insurance revenue for the period is the amount of expected premium receipts (excluding any investment component and adjusted to reflect the time value of money and the effect of financial risk, if applicable, applying paragraph 56) allocated to the period. The entity shall allocate the expected premium receipts to each period of service~~ coverage~~:

(a) ...

...

> Paragraph B128 is amended. New text is underlined and deleted text is struck through.

Insurance finance income or expenses (paragraphs 87–92)

B128 Paragraph 87 requires an entity to include in insurance finance income or expenses the effect of the time value of money and financial risk and changes therein~~ in assumptions that relate to financial risk~~. For the purposes of IFRS 17:

(a) assumptions about inflation based on an index of prices or rates or on prices of assets with inflation-linked returns are assumptions that relate to financial risk;~~ and~~

(b) assumptions about inflation based on an entity's expectation of specific price changes are not assumptions that relate to financial risk; and~~.~~

(c) changes in the measurement of a group of insurance contracts caused by changes in the fair value of underlying items (excluding additions and withdrawals) are changes arising from the effect of the time value of money and financial risk and changes therein.

...

[Draft] Amendments to Appendix C—Effective date and transition

Paragraph C1 is amended. Paragraph C2 is not amended, but is included for ease of reference. New text is underlined and deleted text is struck through.

Effective date

C1 An entity shall apply IFRS 17 for annual reporting periods beginning on or after 1 January 2022 ~~2021~~. If an entity applies IFRS 17 earlier, it shall disclose that fact. Early application is permitted for entities that apply IFRS 9 *Financial Instruments* ~~and IFRS 15 *Revenue from Contracts with Customers*~~ on or before the date of initial application of IFRS 17.

C2 For the purposes of the transition requirements in paragraphs C1 and C3–C33:

(a) the date of initial application is the beginning of the annual reporting period in which an entity first applies IFRS 17; and

(b) the transition date is the beginning of the annual reporting period immediately preceding the date of initial application.

Paragraph C3 is amended and paragraph C5A is added. Paragraph C5 is not amended, but is included for ease of reference. New text is underlined and deleted text is struck through.

Transition

C3 Unless it is impracticable to do so, or paragraph C5A applies, an ~~An~~ entity shall apply IFRS 17 retrospectively ~~unless impracticable~~, except that:

(a) an entity is not required to present the quantitative information required by paragraph 28(f) of IAS 8 *Accounting Policies, Changes in Accounting Estimates and Errors*; and

(b) an entity shall not apply the option in paragraph B115 for periods before the transition date ~~date of initial application~~ of IFRS 17. An entity may apply the option in paragraph B115 prospectively on or after the transition date if, and only if, the entity designates risk mitigation relationships at or before the date it applies the option.

...

C5 If, and only if, it is impracticable for an entity to apply paragraph C3 for a group of insurance contracts, an entity shall apply the following approaches instead of applying paragraph C4(a):

(a) the modified retrospective approach in paragraphs C6–C19, subject to paragraph C6(a); or

(b) the fair value approach in paragraphs C20–C24.

C5A Notwithstanding paragraph C5, an entity may choose to apply the fair value approach in paragraphs C20–C24 for a group of insurance contracts with direct participation features to which it could apply IFRS 17 retrospectively if, and only if:

(a) the entity chooses to apply the risk mitigation option in paragraph B115 to the group of insurance contracts prospectively from the transition date; and

(b) the entity has used derivatives or reinsurance contracts held to mitigate financial risk arising from the group of insurance contracts before the transition date.

Paragraphs C9A and C15A are added. Paragraph C8 is not amended, but is included for ease of reference. New text is underlined.

Modified retrospective approach

...

C8 To achieve the objective of the modified retrospective approach, an entity is permitted to use each modification in paragraphs C9–C19 only to the extent that an entity does not have reasonable and supportable information to apply a retrospective approach.

Assessments at inception or initial recognition

...

C9A To the extent permitted by paragraph C8, an entity shall classify as a liability for incurred claims a liability for settlement of claims incurred before an insurance contract was acquired.

...

Determining the contractual service margin or loss component for groups of insurance contracts without direct participation features

...

C15A For a group of reinsurance contracts held that provides proportionate coverage for an onerous group of insurance contracts and was acquired before or at the same time that the insurance contracts were issued, an entity shall establish a loss-recovery component of the asset for remaining coverage at the transition date (see paragraphs 66A–66B). To the extent permitted by paragraph C8, an entity shall determine the loss-recovery component by multiplying:

(a) the loss component of the liability for remaining coverage for the group of underlying insurance contracts at the transition date (see paragraphs C16 and C20); and

(b) the fixed percentage of claims for the group of underlying insurance contracts the entity has a right to recover from the group of reinsurance contracts held.

...

Paragraphs C20A and C22A are added. New text is underlined.

Fair value approach

...

C20A For a group of reinsurance contracts held to which paragraphs 66A–66B apply at the transition date, an entity shall determine the loss-recovery component of the asset for remaining coverage by multiplying:

(a) the loss component of the liability for remaining coverage for the underlying insurance contracts at the transition date (see paragraphs C16 and C20); and

(b) the fixed percentage of claims for the group of underlying insurance contracts the entity has a right to recover from the group of reinsurance contracts held.

...

C22A In applying the fair value approach, an entity may choose to classify as a liability for incurred claims a liability for settlement of claims incurred before an insurance contract was acquired.

...

[Draft] Amendments to Appendix D—Amendments to other IFRS Standards

...

IFRS 3 *Business Combinations*

In the amendments to IFRS 3 *Business Combinations*, paragraph 64N is amended. New text is underlined and deleted text is struck through.

...

Effective date

...

64N IFRS 17, <u>as amended in [date]</u> ~~issued in May 2017~~, amended paragraphs 17, 20, 21, 35 and B63, and after paragraph 31 added a heading and paragraph 31A. An entity shall apply ~~those~~ <u>the amendments to paragraph 17 to business combinations with an acquisition date after the date of initial application of IFRS 17. An entity shall apply the other</u> amendments when it applies IFRS 17.

...

IFRS 7 *Financial Instruments: Disclosures*

In the amendments to IFRS 7 *Financial Instruments: Disclosures*, paragraphs 3(d) and 44DD are amended. New text is underlined and deleted text is struck through.

Scope

3 This IFRS shall be applied by all entities to all types of financial instruments, except:

(a) ...

(d) <u>insurance contracts as defined in</u> ~~contracts within the scope of~~ IFRS 17 *Insurance Contracts* <u>or investment contracts with discretionary participation features within the scope of IFRS 17</u>. However, this IFRS applies to:

(i) derivatives that are embedded in contracts within the scope of IFRS 17, if IFRS 9 requires the entity to account for them separately<u>.</u>~~; and~~

(ii) investment components that are separated from contracts within the scope of IFRS 17, if IFRS 17 requires such separation<u>, unless the separated investment component is an investment contract with discretionary participation features</u>.

(iii) Moreover, an issuer shall apply this IFRS to *financial guarantee contracts*, if the issuer applies IFRS 9 in recognising and measuring the contracts. However, the issuer, but shall apply IFRS 17 if the issuer elects, in accordance with paragraph 7(e) of IFRS 17, to apply IFRS 17 in recognising and measuring the contracts them.

(iv) credit card contracts an entity issues that meet the definition of an insurance contract but which paragraph 7(h) of IFRS 17 excludes from the scope of IFRS 17 because the entity does not reflect an assessment of the insurance risk associated with an individual customer in setting the price of the contract with that customer.

(v) insurance contracts that an entity issues that limit the compensation for insured events to the amount required to settle the policyholder's obligation created by the contract, if the entity elects, in accordance with paragraph 8A of IFRS 17, to apply IFRS 9 instead of IFRS 17 to such contracts.

(e) ...

...

Effective date and transition

...

40DD IFRS 17, as amended in [date] issued in May 2017, amended paragraphs 3, 8 and 29 and deleted paragraph 30. An entity shall apply those amendments when it applies IFRS 17.

IFRS 9 *Financial Instruments*

In IFRS 9 *Financial Instruments*, paragraphs 2.1 and 7.1.6 are amended. A new heading and paragraphs 7.2.36–7.2.42 are added. New text is underlined and deleted text is struck through.

Chapter 2 Scope

2.1 **This Standard shall be applied by all entities to all types of financial instruments except:**

(a) ...

(e) **rights and obligations arising under an insurance contract as defined in a contract within the scope of IFRS 17 *Insurance Contracts*, other than an issuer's rights and obligations arising under an insurance contract that meets the definition of a financial guarantee contract or an investment contract with discretionary participation features within the scope of IFRS 17. However, this Standard applies to:**

(i) ~~a derivative~~ derivatives that are ~~is~~ embedded in ~~a contract~~ contracts within the scope of IFRS 17, if the ~~derivative~~ derivatives are not themselves ~~is not itself a contract~~ contracts within the scope of IFRS 17.~~; and~~

(ii) ~~an investment component~~ investment components that are ~~is~~ separated from ~~a contract~~ contracts within the scope of IFRS 17, if IFRS 17 requires such separation, unless the separated investment component is an investment contract with discretionary participation features.

(iii) insurance contracts that meet the definition of a financial guarantee contract. However ~~Moreover~~, if an issuer of financial guarantee contracts has previously asserted explicitly that it regards such contracts as insurance contracts and has used accounting that is applicable to insurance contracts, the issuer may elect to apply either this Standard or IFRS 17 to such financial guarantee contracts (see paragraphs B2.5–B2.6). The issuer may make that election contract by contract, but the election for each contract is irrevocable.

(iv) credit card contracts an entity issues that meet the definition of an insurance contract but which paragraph 7(h) of IFRS 17 excludes from the scope of IFRS 17 because the entity does not reflect an assessment of the insurance risk associated with an individual customer in setting the price of the contract with that customer.

(v) insurance contracts that an entity issues that limit the compensation for insured events to the amount required to settle the policyholder's obligation created by the contract, if the entity elects, in accordance with paragraph 8A of IFRS 17, to apply IFRS 9 instead of IFRS 17 to such contracts.

(f) ...

...

Chapter 7 Effective date and transition

7.1 Effective date

...

7.1.6 IFRS 17, as amended in [date], ~~issued in May 2017,~~ amended paragraphs 2.1, B2.1, B2.4, B2.5 and B4.1.30, and added paragraphs ~~paragraph~~ 3.3.5 and 7.2.36–7.2.42. An entity shall apply those amendments when it applies IFRS 17.

...

7.2 Transition

...

Transition for IFRS 17 as amended in [date]

7.2.36 An entity shall apply the amendments to IFRS 9 made by IFRS 17 as amended in [date] retrospectively in accordance with IAS 8, except as specified in paragraphs 7.2.37–7.2.42.

7.2.37 An entity that first applies IFRS 17 as amended in [date] at the same time it first applies this Standard shall apply paragraphs 7.2.1–7.2.28 instead of paragraphs 7.2.38–7.2.42.

7.2.38 An entity that first applies IFRS 17 as amended in [date] after it first applies this Standard shall apply paragraphs 7.2.39–7.2.42. The entity shall also apply the other transition requirements in this Standard necessary for applying these amendments. For that purpose, references to the date of initial application shall be read as referring to the beginning of the reporting period in which an entity first applies these amendments (date of initial application of these amendments).

7.2.39 With regard to designating a financial liability as measured at fair value through profit or loss, an entity:

(a) shall revoke its previous designation of a financial liability as measured at fair value through profit or loss if that designation was previously made in accordance with the condition in paragraph 4.2.2(a) but that condition is no longer satisfied as a result of the application of these amendments; and

(b) may designate a financial liability as measured at fair value through profit or loss if that designation would not have previously satisfied the condition in paragraph 4.2.2(a) but that condition is now satisfied as a result of the application of these amendments.

Such a designation and revocation shall be made on the basis of the facts and circumstances that exist at the date of initial application of these amendments. That classification shall be applied retrospectively.

7.2.40 An entity is not required to restate prior periods to reflect the application of these amendments. The entity may restate prior periods only if it is possible to do so without the use of hindsight. If an entity restates prior periods, the restated financial statements must reflect all the requirements in this Standard for the affected financial instruments. If an entity does not restate prior periods, the entity shall recognise any difference between the previous carrying amount and the carrying amount at the beginning of the annual reporting period that includes the date of initial application of these amendments in the opening retained earnings (or other component of equity, as appropriate) of the annual reporting period that includes the date of initial application of these amendments.

7.2.41 In the reporting period that includes the date of initial application of these amendments, an entity is not required to present the quantitative information required by paragraph 28(f) of IAS 8.

7.2.42 In the reporting period that includes the date of initial application of these amendments, the entity shall disclose the following information as at that date of initial application for each class of financial assets and financial liabilities that were affected by these amendments:

(a) the previous classification, including the previous measurement category when applicable, and carrying amount determined immediately before applying these amendments;

(b) the new measurement category and carrying amount determined after applying these amendments;

(c) the carrying amount of any financial liabilities in the statement of financial position that were previously designated as measured at fair value through profit or loss but are no longer so designated; and

(d) the reasons for any designation or de-designation of financial liabilities as measured at fair value through profit or loss.

IAS 1 *Presentation of Financial Statements*

In the amendments to IAS 1 *Presentation of Financial Statements* paragraphs 54(da), 54(ma) and 139R are amended. New text is underlined and deleted text is struck through.

Information to be presented in the statement of financial position

54 **The statement of financial position shall include line items that present the following amounts:**

(a) ...

(da) **portfolios ~~groups~~ of contracts within the scope of IFRS 17 that are assets, disaggregated as required by paragraph 78 of IFRS 17;**

...

(ma) **portfolios ~~groups~~ of contracts within the scope of IFRS 17 that are liabilities, disaggregated as required by paragraph 78 of IFRS 17;**

...

Transition and effective date

...

139R IFRS 17, as amended in [date] ~~issued in May 2017~~, amended paragraphs 7, 54 and 82. An entity shall apply those amendments when it applies IFRS 17.

...

IAS 32 *Financial Instruments: Presentation*

In the amendments to IAS 32 *Financial Instruments: Presentation* paragraphs 4(d) and 97T are amended. New text is underlined and deleted text is struck through.

Scope

4 **This Standard shall be applied by all entities to all types of financial instruments except:**

(a) …

(d) insurance contracts as defined in ~~contracts within the scope of~~ IFRS 17 *Insurance Contracts* or investment contracts with discretionary participation features within the scope of IFRS 17. However, this Standard applies to:

(i) derivatives that are embedded in contracts within the scope of IFRS 17, if IFRS 9 requires the entity to account for them separately.~~; and~~

(ii) investment components that are separated from contracts within the scope of IFRS 17, if IFRS 17 requires such separation, unless the separated investment component is an investment contract with discretionary participation features.

(iii) ~~Moreover, an issuer shall apply this Standard to~~ financial guarantee contracts, if the issuer applies IFRS 9 in recognising and measuring the contracts. However, the issuer~~, but~~ shall apply IFRS 17 if the issuer elects, in accordance with paragraph 7(e) of IFRS 17, to apply IFRS 17 in recognising and measuring the contracts ~~them~~.

(iv) credit card contracts an entity issues that meet the definition of an insurance contract but which paragraph 7(h) of IFRS 17 excludes from the scope of IFRS 17 because the entity does not reflect an assessment of the insurance risk associated with an individual customer in setting the price of the contract with that customer.

(v) insurance contracts that an entity issues that limit the compensation for insured events to the amount required to settle the policyholder's obligation created by the contract if the entity elects, in accordance with paragraph 8A of IFRS 17, to apply IFRS 9 instead of IFRS 17 to such contracts.

…

Effective date and transition

...

97T IFRS 17, as amended in [date] ~~issued in May 2017~~, amended paragraphs 4, AG8 and AG36, and added paragraph 33A. An entity shall apply those amendments when it applies IFRS 17.

[Draft] Amendments to Illustrative Examples on IFRS 17

Illustrative Example 19 is added. In addition, the Board expects to make any necessary consequential amendments to the Illustrative Examples accompanying IFRS 17 if it finalises the proposals in Exposure Draft *Amendments to IFRS 17*.

Example 19—Measurement of a group of reinsurance contracts held that provides proportionate coverage for groups of underlying insurance contracts, including an onerous group (paragraphs 66A–66B and B119C–B119F)

IE200 This example illustrates the initial and subsequent measurement of reinsurance contracts held that provide proportionate coverage, when a group of underlying insurance contracts is onerous.

Assumptions

IE201 At the beginning of Year 1, an entity enters into a reinsurance contract that in return for a fixed premium covers 30 per cent of each claim from the groups of underlying insurance contracts. The underlying insurance contracts are issued at the beginning of Year 1.

IE202 In this example for simplicity it is assumed:

(a) no contracts will lapse before the end of the coverage period;

(b) there are no changes in estimates other than that described in paragraph IE209; and

(c) all other amounts, including the effect of discounting, the risk adjustments for non-financial risk, and the risk of non-performance of the reinsurer are ignored.

IE203 Some of the underlying insurance contracts are onerous at initial recognition. Thus, applying paragraph 16, the entity establishes a group comprising the onerous contracts. The remainder of the underlying insurance contracts are expected to be profitable and applying paragraph 16, in this example, the entity establishes a single group comprising the profitable contracts.

IE204 The coverage period of the underlying insurance contracts and the reinsurance contract held is three years starting from the beginning of Year 1. Service is provided evenly across the coverage periods.

IE205 The entity expects to receive premiums of CU1,110 on the underlying insurance contracts immediately after initial recognition. Claims on the underlying insurance contracts are expected to be incurred evenly across the coverage period and are paid immediately after the claims are incurred.

IE206 The entity measures the groups of underlying insurance contracts on initial recognition as follows:

	Profitable group of insurance contracts	Onerous group of insurance contracts	Total
	CU	CU	CU
Estimates of present value of future cash inflows	(900)	(210)	(1,110)
Estimates of present value of future cash outflows	600	300	900
Fulfilment cash flows	(300)	90	(210)
Contractual service margin	300	-	300
Insurance contract liability on initial recognition	-	**90**	**90**
Loss on initial recognition	-	**(90)**	**(90)**

IE207 Applying paragraph 61, the entity establishes a group comprising a single reinsurance contract held that provides proportionate coverage. The entity pays a premium of CU315 to the reinsurer immediately after initial recognition. The entity expects to receive recoveries of claims from the reinsurer on the same day that the entity pays claims on the underlying insurance contracts.

IE208 Applying paragraph 63, the entity measures the estimates of the present value of the future cash flows for the group of reinsurance contracts held using assumptions consistent with those used to measure the estimates of the present value of the future cash flows for the groups of underlying insurance contracts. Consequently, the estimate of the present value of the future cash inflows is CU270 (recovery of 30 per cent of the estimates of the present value of the future cash outflows for the groups of underlying insurance contracts of CU900).

IE209 At the end of Year 2, the entity revises its estimates of the remaining fulfilment cash outflows of the groups of underlying insurance contracts. The entity estimates that the fulfilment cash flows of the groups of underlying insurance contracts increase by 10 per cent, from future cash outflows of CU300 to future cash outflows of CU330. Consequently, the entity estimates the fulfilment cash flows of the reinsurance contract held also increase, from future cash inflows of CU90 to future cash inflows of CU99.

Analysis

IE210 The entity measures the group of reinsurance contracts held on initial recognition as follows:

	Initial recognition	
	CU	
Estimates of present value of future cash inflows (recoveries)	(270)	
Estimates of present value of future cash outflows (premiums)	315	
Fulfilment cash flows	45	
Contractual service margin of the reinsurance contract held (before the loss-recovery adjustment)	(45)	
Loss-recovery component	(27)	(a)
Contractual service margin of the reinsurance contract held (after the loss-recovery adjustment)	(72)	(b)
Reinsurance contract asset on initial recognition	**(27)**	(c)
Income on initial recognition	**27**	(a)

(a) Applying paragraph 66A [of this Exposure Draft], the entity adjusts the contractual service margin of the reinsurance contract held and recognises income to reflect the loss recovery. Applying paragraph B119D [of this Exposure Draft] the entity determines the adjustment to the contractual service margin and the income recognised as CU27 (the loss of CU90 recognised for the onerous group of underlying insurance contracts multiplied by 30 per cent, the fixed percentage of claims the entity has the right to recover).

(b) The contractual service margin of CU45 is adjusted by CU27, resulting in a contractual service margin of CU72, reflecting a net cost on the reinsurance contract held.

(c) The reinsurance contract asset of CU27 comprises the fulfilment cash flows of CU45 (net outflows) and a contractual service margin reflecting a net cost of CU72. Applying paragraph 66B [of this Exposure Draft], the entity establishes a loss-recovery component of the asset for remaining coverage of CU27 depicting the recovery of losses recognised applying paragraph 66A [of this Exposure Draft].

IE211 At the end of Year 1, the entity measures the insurance contract liability and the reinsurance contract asset as follows:

	Insurance contract liability		Reinsurance contract asset
	Profitable group of insurance contracts	Onerous group of insurance contracts	
	CU	CU	CU
Estimates of present value of future cash inflows (recoveries)	-	-	(180)
Estimates of present value of future cash outflows (claims)	400	200	-
Fulfilment cash flows	400	200	(180)
Contractual service margin	200	-	(48)
Insurance contract liability	**600**	**200**	
Reinsurance contract asset			**(228)**

IE212 At the end of Year 2, the entity measures the insurance contract liability and the reinsurance contract asset as follows:

	Insurance contract liability		Reinsurance contract asset
	Profitable group of insurance contracts	Onerous group of insurance contracts	
	CU	CU	CU
Estimates of present value of future cash inflows (recoveries)	-	-	(99) (a)
Estimates of present value of future cash outflows (claims)	220 (a)	110 (a)	-
Fulfilment cash flows	220	110	(99)
Contractual service margin	90 (b)	-	(21) (e)
Insurance contract liability	**310**	**110**	
Reinsurance contract asset			**(120)**
Recognition of loss and recovery of loss		**(10)** (c)	**3** (d)

continued...

...continued

(a) The entity increases the expected remaining cash outflows of the groups of underlying insurance contracts by 10 per cent for each group (CU30 in total) and increases the expected remaining cash inflows of the reinsurance contract held by 10 per cent of the expected recoveries of CU90 (CU9).

(b) Applying paragraph 44(c), the entity adjusts the carrying amount of the contractual service margin of CU200 by CU20 for the changes in fulfilment cash flows relating to future service. Applying paragraph 44(e), the entity also adjusts the carrying amount of the contractual service margin by CU90 for the amount recognised as insurance revenue ((CU200 - CU20 = CU180) ÷ 2). The resulting contractual service margin at the end of year 2 is CU90 (CU200 - CU20 - CU90).

(c) Applying paragraph 48, the entity recognises in profit or loss an amount of CU10 for the changes in the fulfilment cash flows relating to future services of the onerous group of underlying insurance contracts.

(d) Applying paragraph 66(c)(ii), the entity adjusts the contractual service margin of the reinsurance contract held for the change in fulfilment cash flows that relate to future service unless the change results from a change in fulfilment cash flows allocated to a group of underlying insurance contracts that does not adjust the contractual service margin for that group. Consequently, the entity recognises the change in the fulfilment cash flows of the reinsurance contract held of CU9 by:

   (i) recognising immediately in profit or loss CU3 of the change in the fulfilment cash flows of the reinsurance contract held (30 per cent of the CU10 change in the fulfilment cash flows of the onerous group of underlying insurance contracts that does not adjust the contractual service margin of those contracts); and

   (ii) adjusting the contractual service margin of the reinsurance contract held by CU6 of the change in the fulfilment cash flows (CU9 - CU3).

(e) Consequently, the contractual service margin of the reinsurance contract held of CU(21) equals the contractual service margin at the end of Year 1 of CU(48) adjusted for CU6 and for CU21 of the contractual service margin recognised for the service received in Year 2 (CU(21) = (CU(48) + CU6) ÷ 2).

[Draft] Amendments to Basis for Conclusions on IFRS 17

A footnote is added to the end of paragraph BC265 of the Basis for Conclusions on IFRS 17 as follows.

* When developing the [proposed] amendments to IFRS 17, the Board observed that not all entities that may be described as mutual entities have the feature that the most residual interest of the entity is due to a policyholder.

A footnote is added to the end of paragraph BC304 of the Basis for Conclusions on IFRS 17 as follows.

* Paragraphs BC304 and BC305 describe reinsurance contracts held that cover aggregate losses over a specified amount arising from a group of insurance contracts. When developing the [proposed] amendments to IFRS 17, the Board observed that if a reinsurance contract held covers claims in excess of a specified amount on an individual insurance contract, that reinsurance contract does not provide proportionate coverage.

[Draft] Amendments to IFRS 4 *Insurance Contracts*

In IFRS 4 *Insurance Contracts*, paragraphs 20A, 20J and 20O are amended. New text is underlined and deleted text is struck through.

Temporary exemption from IFRS 9

20A **IFRS 9 addresses the accounting for financial instruments and is effective for annual periods beginning on or after 1 January 2018. However, for an insurer that meets the criteria in paragraph 20B, this IFRS provides a temporary exemption that permits, but does not require, the insurer to apply IAS 39 *Financial Instruments: Recognition and Measurement* rather than IFRS 9 for annual periods beginning before 1 January 2022 ~~2021~~. An insurer that applies the temporary exemption from IFRS 9 shall:**

(a) ...

...

20J If an entity no longer qualifies for the temporary exemption from IFRS 9 as a result of a reassessment (see paragraph 20G(a)), then the entity is permitted to continue to apply the temporary exemption from IFRS 9 only until the end of the annual period that began immediately after that reassessment. Nevertheless, the entity must apply IFRS 9 for annual periods beginning on or after 1 January 2022 ~~2021~~. For example, if an entity determines that it no longer qualifies for the temporary exemption from IFRS 9 applying paragraph 20G(a) on 31 December 2018 (the end of its annual period), then the entity is permitted to continue to apply the temporary exemption from IFRS 9 only until 31 December 2019.

...

Temporary exemption from specific requirements in IAS 28

20O Paragraphs 35–36 of IAS 28 *Investments in Associates and Joint Ventures* require an entity to apply uniform accounting policies when using the equity method. Nevertheless, for annual periods beginning before 1 January 2022 ~~2021~~, an entity is permitted, but not required, to retain the relevant accounting policies applied by the associate or joint venture as follows:

(a) ...

Approval by the International Accounting Standards Board of Exposure Draft *Amendments to IFRS 17* published in June 2019

This Exposure Draft *Amendments to IFRS 17* was approved for publication by 14 of the 14 members of the International Accounting Standards Board.

Hans Hoogervorst	Chairman
Suzanne Lloyd	Vice-Chair
Nick Anderson	
Martin Edelmann	
Françoise Flores	
Amaro Luiz de Oliveira Gomes	
Gary Kabureck	
Jianqiao Lu	
Takatsugu Ochi	
Darrel Scott	
Tom Scott	
Chungwoo Suh	
Ann Tarca	
Mary Tokar	